RESTORE OLD PATHS

Karen Kellock Ph.D.

Manual for Superior Men

A complete theory based on Einstein physics,
Political Psychology, Systems Theory
and Archetypal Psychiatry.

FORMULA

All success attraction
All disease obstruction
All recovery elimination

You must fast on all three

OBSTRUCTIONS:

People
Habit
Food

RESTORE OLD PATHS

The cruel beasts known as the Philistines are impervious to beauty, gross, mean.   The false kings collude together against one and such toxic ties can often become trauma bonds: picture yourself cutting em then feeling the exhilaration.   Typically a scapegoat is not aware people are gossiping 'til years later on.   How can you get back at someone who's dead? Eventually we must forgive instead.

JUST PAY EM OFF

USERS: JUST PAY EM OFF
GOD REMOVES PEOPLE
YOUR SEASON ABOVE FOOLS
LET THE IMMATURE GO
YOU CAN'T HANDLE EM
GO BEYOND HATERS FROM PAST
DIET TIPS FOR DAILY FASTERS
ALTERNATE DAILY MEALS
NOTE THE CONTRADICTIONS
MAKE YOUR OWN REALITY FUN

JUST PAY EM OFF

USERS: JUST PAY EM OFF

With the users in your life it's best to just pay them off. Get rid of em to start anew with big payoff.

I paid off a user when he didn't deserve it but the next day it all opened up for me, believe it.

Getting rid of people is such a shot in the arm it's good to pay em off tho' you'd rather do em harm.

Tho' they rejected and did you dirty that last day, it cleared the way for the arrival of destiny.

You're too mature for people who refused to see your light and value so God had their removal.

GOD REMOVES PEOPLE

There is no way God could prosper you but by isolating you by yourself, away from the "cool".

They saw something in you so they attracted in and huddled around, bringing their friends too.

Because you didn't take CONTROL at this point you were brought down by the inferiors ok?

You let them have their way so they bought YOUR way down to the ground, losing your destiny.

You've got to have the strength and guts to draw lines, though of course they'll call you unkind.

You're the superior man or woman, not them. Draw lines or they'll bring you down friends.

JUST PAY EM OFF

I didn't have the guts to draw lines so my life was debased for decades. Be strong or die ok.

Your newfound maturity brings a new season with God. Christ is about drawing lines not just "love".

You no longer go out with people causing chaos. That's all it is: ANARCHY with partying & loudness.

You no longer fit in with the crowd but do the Lord's work for YOUR life: He plans your steps, aye.

YOUR SEASON ABOVE FOOLS

This is your season of rising above the foolishness and immaturity of your generation, amen?

Even a little bit of absurdity you can't give into. You must state the case & cast em out too.

We've been marching into hell since the sixties and now we're being ruled by eighty year old hippies.

Weakened, I fell into my bag: of addictions to deal with em and slowly but surely became an old hag.

When I bravely stood up to the crowd I got my youth back. You must or lose God's help in fact.

Christianity is not about "loving everybody" but drawing lines. Most can't do that: the cowards, aye.

People don't grow from situations, they only get worse. But you got stronger, overcoming the curse.

Once hurt and debased, they caused havoc in other's lives but you chose to help others, aye.

LET THE IMMATURE GO

JUST PAY EM OFF

Let immature people [no matter their age] watch you from a distance cuz they are like a virus.

Immature thinking makes you mad and you just can't afford that: anxiety up, reality goes black.

You're an interesting person but will lose that uniqueness when adapting to un-reason.

Watch who comes in your home. That's your personal space not a hangout for just anyone.

YOU CAN'T HANDLE EM

Just when you start to get peace you think you can handle em but you can't: no time for dumb.

Tho' they brag on their high IQ their notions are dumbed down, having nothing to offer you.

Focus on the Lord for your life your highness, not these individuals wanting to stop your progress.

The way Trump is misjudged for his actions every day is exactly what happens to you when TRUE ok.

Block em or ignore their call cuz you got better things to do then be bored/brought down y'all.

Ignore their foolishness because they gotta get right with God just like you did facing His rod.

Some of these clowns are in their 80's since maturity has absolutely nothing to do with age see.

If they refuse to get right with God then hit the block button. You're too mature for the herd hon'.

GO BEYOND HATERS FROM PAST

JUST PAY EM OFF

Go way beyond haters from your past or people who just don't like you. Ignore and block em Sue.

It's good to get wisdom from elderly people but a lot of them are just as dumb, being liberals.

Watch who you seek for knowledge and counsel. Watch out for old hippies who are so full of bull.

While walking in your new season of maturity ask the holy spirit who's right for you or really pay.

DIET TIPS FOR DAILY FASTERS

Now remember: one delicious meal then flying high all day, taking anything that comes your way.

Sensitivity can be bad as depression & panic attacks come easily but food control calms it see.

A terror/depression would hit but since I took control after breakfast this hasn't happened sis.

With food plans like one meal a day your moods are controlled too. Try it and see this soon.

One meal then you KNOW you're in fasting consciousness and that it'll be a bright day sis.

There's nothing WRONG with self-control. It's a fruit of the spirit but anorexics are blamed for it.

Most people have NO control. They're subject to whims and impulses: just look in their shopping carts.

I made a list of eight things I ate, never to deviate: No more trying things only to feel stuffed later ok.

ALTERNATE DAILY MEALS

JUST PAY EM OFF

The hypersensitive must alternate days, e.g.: spaghetti [8 oz], tacos [4] or potatoes with avocado ok.

You can think of it as the acid-alkaline diet or the starch solution diet, another way to see it.

Whole continents exist on starch: beans, corn, wheat or rice and they're energetic and thin, aye.

I'm 5'3" & 96 pounds: perfect for me. The Asian female body type is 20 lbs lighter than American fatties.

I'm not Asian but the fact a lower weight is normal for some is enough for me to accept it hon'.

NOTE THE CONTRADICTIONS

Fingernail contradictions: we "need protein" [acid] but stomach acid breaks and splinters them.

For fingernail integrity and strength, we need alkaline but that means no protein: it's a mix up see.

These total contradictions in diet science mean you gotta just try it. Trial and error decides it.

Before you know it, life is over. You must enjoy your latter years and diet solutions are solvers.

Isolation, rigid routines and lists mark the mature anorexic though "they" say they mark the sick.

Asian noodles with peas & corn would be neutral. Alternate with spaghetti, tacos and potatoes.

Butter is considered a neutral food [POE] but with spuds I gained weight: they're plugs.

Alternating meals is essential for the chemically sensitive. Since allergy sets in, we just gotta do it.

JUST PAY EM OFF

MAKE YOUR OWN REALITY FUN

Don't put fun on a pedestal--vacationing, partying, eating--cuz you gotta come down from it all.

Make your OWN reality where it's at because then you don't have to come down from that.

DIET CHAT

ALKALINE DIET FOR DE-AGING
CHECK ALKALINE ON INTERNET
SEE WHAT WORKS
VANITY IS VERY HEALTHY
WRINKLED ARMS AND LEGS
BEAUTY REPLACES DESIRE
GO ALKALINE AND DE-AGE
FRUITARIANISM: FAILURE TO THRIVE
REDMON'S SALT FOR MINERALS
EXPECT TIREDNESS FOR TWO DAYS
FRUITARIANISM WAS TOO EXTREME
DIFFERENT FROM THE MONSTER TRIBE
YOUTHFUL BEAUTY WILL RETURN
ONE MEAL: A STEAK A DAY?
FASTING CONSCIOUSNESS IS KEY
DON'T FRET INCREASED ISOLATION

DIET FOR YOUTH/BEAUTY

ALKALINE DIET FOR DE-AGING

Design your own diet. Keep it all alkaline but besides that, don't listen to anyone and just do it.

Go all alkaline and be amazed as all wrinkles leave the body. No matter what age, it's all beauty.

She looked ninety as the skin hung in wrinkled folds but went alkaline and it came back [not old].

You don't have to go all fruit to do it. Eat cauliflower, salsa, avocado and lettuce to be cute.

Eat what YOU want/how you want it but keep it all alkaline: fruits/veggies and almonds are fine.

CHECK ALKALINE ON INTERNET

Check out all foods on the internet: is it alkaline or low acid? Just eat that and look fabulous.

If you want a little cheese on it, fine: you can neutralize acidic foods with your veggies for alkaline.

I substituted tortillas with veggies and it was just as delicious. Salsa, guacamole and my lettuce.

ALL wrinkles left the body and I couldn't have been more happy. I guess I'm just vain you see.

I was mis-advised to use PROTEIN to de-wrinkle the body but that made it even more wrinkly.

If you want protein, cheese is as high as meat see. Go ahead & add it but you won't be wrinkle free.

DIET FOR YOUTH AND BEAUTY

Fruitarians eventually fail to thrive. It works fine at first but with depletion you'll desire more, aye.

I tried living on grapes and cantaloupes. It just wasn't enough but I was satisfied with vegetables.

SEE WHAT WORKS

Add some cheese and see if it works. You're still low acid and it's a good transition at first.

Suddenly I felt so good in the morning. A whole new reality was dawning as my body was youthing.

Alkaline: fruits, veggies, almonds and seeds. All else [animal/processed food] goes acid see.

As skin hung in folds and I really looked old I stopped smoking pot too and de-aged [made gold!]

All processed food [grains, pasta, all of it] goes acid. When I suddenly de-aged I didn't want any of it.

I tried eating my favorite acid foods [Mexican, Italian] just once a day but still had wrinkles ok.

VANITY IS VERY HEALTHY

It all depends how vain you are. Can you be happy looking that way or do you wanna be a star?

I couldn't believe how it all smoothed out in a couple days. Tell the world: alkaline is the only way.

Acid foods: wake up depressed & nervous. Alkaline: look at the moon, enjoy the sun: joyous!

If you wanna go fruitarian, try it for awhile. You may be one who can restrict for major style.

DIET FOR YOUTH AND BEAUTY

If I have fruit for breakfast I wanna eat again all day. I want ONE meal then just work/fast today.

I tried the carnivore diet to de-wrinkle the body. That's when obvious aging happened suddenly.

Look up "alkaline diet and winkles": you don't see that much on it. But it's true, believe and try it.

WRINKLED ARMS AND LEGS

Usually skinny and older means wrinkled arms and legs [uglier]. You can be twelve again & prettier.

I couldn't believe a loving God would make us so ugly when old so going alkaline I made gold.

Ultimately what brings us to Godly reality is the saints choose BEAUTY but this isn't just vanity.

Skin hanging in wrinkles and folds: This ISN'T what it means to grow old and alkaline proves gold.

BEAUTY REPLACES DESIRE

I was so relieved and delighted I lost all desire for animal foods [eggs, meat and butter] in my diet.

As long as it all stays alkaline that's all that matters. Don't take advice on diet other than that sir.

It's all so simple, just check out the charts. That's all you do for youth: God's food is in charge.

Shrimp is on the cusp: it's neutral. Things like that give you leeway on what to eat when out too.

Some fish in restaurants: very low acid so that's what you eat and you'll still look like a debutante.

DIET FOR YOUTH AND BEAUTY

Check out the charts and learn it all well. That's all you need for life: vitality, energy, looking swell.

Acid foods: [animal/all processed] and look your age or older. Alkaline foods: de-age/be much cuter.

GO ALKALINE AND DE-AGE

Go alkaline, de-age, be wise: you'll see everyone differently, discerning what they eat, aye.

Everyone said to eat more protein, they all said that! But that didn't help, the skin still fell flat.

I went alkaline and was a cute young chick again. I'm telling you this is it: a major insight friends!

I took rice, pasta & grains to the food bank. I replaced it all with raisins & almonds: God, thanks!

For years I said fruitarianism was the only way to do it. I was famished for acid foods, it just wasn't.

Fruit is great but raisins [the most alkaline] fills the bill. They don't perish and I'm even cuter still.

Macaroni and cheese: I can't think of anything more acidifying, depleting and uglifying see.

FRUITARIANISM: FAILURE TO THRIVE

Fruitarianism: fine is you can do it. I tried it for years and couldn't sustain it/wanted more in diet.

Fruit dilapidates in the frig if you don't eat it right away. Raisins keep for years/can be stored ok.

Black olives are another alkalinizing food. They're delicious with your guacamole dudes.

DIET FOR YOUTH AND BEAUTY

After delicious breakfast is digested, in the afternoons I eat almonds & raisins, thanking heaven.

The body rebels when eating acid foods, reacting with mucus, the ultimate uglyfier & depleter too.

Alkaline foods BIND and take out the mucus, giving great relief from this devil causing disease.

NOW you'll be happy and young, waking up carefree & enjoying life more than any spending spree.

Ehretists say to skip breakfast but I couldn't do that. I wanna eat then work all day in a happy fast.

People used to eat a big breakfast then work all day in the fields. Just skip dinner to feel unreal.

Some say to go "all raw" but that also didn't work for me. Cooked is still alkaline and delicious see.

I wanna eat once then be in fasting consciousness all day. Working and not thinking of food ok.

REDMON'S SALT FOR MINERALS

If you wanna salt your veggies, use Redmon's. it's actually minerals so no more worryin'.

If you wanna use parmasan on your veggies, go for it. Don't get compulsive with this, enjoy it.

Don't listen to "don't eat this, eat that" kinda stuff. As long as it's ALKALINE that's all you want.

RELAX with your diet or you'll go off of it. This is pure enjoyment and you'll look so good on it.

If you wanna skip breakfast, go all raw & only eat fruit, go for it. Don't listen to me either on diet.

DIET FOR YOUTH AND BEAUTY

Alkaline noodles, Japanese Ramen is fine. Corn tortillas are on the line, have fish occasionally, aye.

Cheese/fish is a little acid so balance with veggies. Always strive to neutralize then relax see.

EXPECT TIREDNESS FOR TWO DAYS

Expect tiredness the first couple days. After all, you've been acid for years so the system pays.

I'm delighted that corn tortillas are about neutral. I love tacos so alternate days with noodles.

Potatoes are alkaline and filing I love em with avocado so this diet has variety and never boring.

Just recall animal foods and processed are the acids, but it isn't vegan, have fish if you like it.

Flavorings like soy sauce are mildly acid but it's all about balancing things so you can use it.

FRUITARIANISM WAS TOO EXTREME

When first learning of acid-alkaline I went to the extreme as a "fruitarian" but it didn't last see.

Striking for a middle ground as outlined above made the diet lasting and I was as happy as a dove.

Happiness is the true measure of success. Many rich are unhappy and their lives are a mess.

All you need is one good meal and a snack. Make the meal alkaline & enjoy raisins/nuts in the aft.

On the fourth day, all the wrinkles are gone! You'll buy only ALKALINE pasta/noodles from now on.

DIET FOR YOUTH AND BEAUTY

It's an amazing discovery: all your wrinkles are gone! I can't stop saying it: age is irrelevant hon'.

Caveat: With STRESS the wrinkles will come back. You must stay relaxed & calm, I've gotta say that.

The alkalized lady is relaxed, calm and poised. She is a true sophisticate and won't tolerate noise.

Everything will now seem smooth. Not just your skin but your joints and movements too.

It happens simultaneously: you won't crave foods that make you old and ugly anymore, you'll see.

Everyone's eating animal, processed or fast foods and that accounts for their awful looks too.

DIFFERENT FROM THE MONSTER TRIBE

This will differentiate you from the monster tribe. Now you stand out as you should as chosen, aye.

Now remember, just raisins and almonds later. You'll now be skipping lunch and dinner.

Now your spouse will be so proud of you. He'll compare you to the others and know he's lucky too.

You CAN control your destiny. By working harder than anyone else and making right choices see.

You'll see heaven is not a place like Paris or Rome but wise decisions for your food or home.

You'll see paradise is not a vacation or wealth but what you put in your body for energy/beauty/youth.

Have your organic spaghetti with fresh salsa rather than cooked sauce: it is absolutely delicious.

DIET FOR YOUTH AND BEAUTY

So what if you have parmesan on top of your spaghetti--you've balanced it with fresh salsa see.

So you went a little too acid for breakfast--you've balanced it with raisins & nuts in the aft.

YOUTHFUL BEAUTY WILL RETURN

As you see lost youth returning and beauty blooming you'll thank God for His food-creating.

I just don't wanna eat dead animals. I'm sorry but it never occurs to me to buy meat after all.

I don't judge it, you can have your carnivore budget. I just can't do it though the bible allows it.

Meat is HIGHLY acidic. People lose a lot of weight on it so if that's all you care about, go for it.

But the saints choose beauty ultimately and eye-bags and wrinkles are just not it unfortunately.

ONE MEAL: A STEAK A DAY?

There are those who eat one meal: a steak a day. That's fine, don't judge it but with beauty they'll pay.

Organic whole wheat spaghetti with fresh salsa and parmesan: a most delicious breakfast man.

Tacos or spaghetti was all I EVER wanted as a youth. This diet will be easy and delicious too.

Eat your meal by 8-9 a.m. then when hungry [about five hours later] have your raisins and almonds.

Europeans have sweet rolls in the morning for then they have the whole day for it's full digesting.

DIET FOR YOUTH AND BEAUTY

The stupidest thing is to have a big dinner. Eat early for complete digestion: now you'll be a winner.

You eat, then you don't: You have breakfast then work tirelessly without desire [you're whole].

FASTING CONSCIOUSNESS IS KEY

I love fasting consciousness all day. When the rest of the world is down in the gut you're a star ok.

Tea is alkaline. I love having iced tea all day but never coffee or soft drinks even the diet kind ok.

Remember to look it all up and check your sources. Some are so outdated it's very humorous.

Even if you mess up for breakfast, recall it balances out in the afternoon with your almonds/raisins.

Goodbye for now and have a good day. You will if making right food choices for very high-pay.

A good housekeeper cleans when she sees a need, a bad one sees but ignores it for now--please!

They have amnesia on how they treated you--like karma won't affect em--but forgive em anyway Sue.

It is udder-ly ridiculous how women have those big breasts popping out from implants sis.

Don't ever be jealous of other people but have gratitude for your own life and stay free of evil.

DON'T FRET INCREASED ISOLATION

Temptation resisted is the true measure of character. Just say no and with each time it's easier.

DIET FOR YOUTH AND BEAUTY

Don't fret over your increased isolation. It's a sign you're about to burst on the scene with fame hon'.

Always think: INVERSION. If you're broke you'll soon have money, if alone you'll soon have a party.

You're all alone cuz you're CHOSEN. God takes out people [who come & go-- you don't need em].

Alone with God: He wants your total reliance on Him only and that means miracles [awed].

THE MATURE ANOREXIC

ANOREXIA: FULL PHOBIA
BREAKFAST ONLY FOR THE SAINTS
THE FIRST WAKE UP
ROUTINE TRANSGRESSION
OUR FIRST FOOD ADAPTATIONS
MATURITY IS BALANCE
THE FALLACY OF E.D. CLINICS
TO ANOREXICS, A SPECIAL CLASS:
TO FAT COUNSELORS IN ED CLINICS
TAKE THIS ADVICE AND BE HAPPY

THE MATURE ANOREXIC

ANOREXIA: FULL PHOBIA

The anorexic feels like a powerhouse when empty but with fullness anxiety, that's the syndrome see.

Fear of fullness is the main characteristic of anorexics. It brings depression, anxiety and panic.

When she's empty she feels lightheaded, spiritual, energetic and awake. When full it's hell ok.

Low weight on the scales brings elation, a sense of. accomplishment. High weight is tragic.

Low weight and emptiness is a powerhouse of an eternal reality. It's elation and being happy.

Feeling over-full brings a panic and wanting to call 911. It's an emergency of feeling death coming on.

BREAKFAST ONLY FOR THE SAINTS

The mature anorexic learns to eat break-fast only. She does her writing, eats then flies off to eternity.

Eat again and fullness fear takes over. She has to take Benadryl or some other calmer, all bummers.

If she eats once and not again she wakes up thin and energetic, ready to be a powerhouse/quick.

Her friends pray for her when they see her routine. They don't see it as the best they've ever seen.

This anorexic routine is like an amphetamine, putting her on a elation trip all day you see [free].

THE MATURE ANOREXIC

The immature anorexic uses purging to do it. This is a disgusting thing [must mature beyond it].

If emptiness brings elation and fullness brings panic and depression the young choose purgation.

Eating again after breakfast feels like a complete failure. Never again she thinks, becoming mature.

They all want her to eat lunch or dinner. Gradually she flies free of these losers from the culture.

THE FIRST WAKE UP

Waking up after a successful one-meal routine the previous day is ELATION: it is heaven ok.

A mature anorexic makes it to old age while the immature die early in utter tragedy ok.

One meal a day: "I can see clearly now". Eating again after breakfast: "life is hell and misery": wow.

One meal and maybe a snack: raisins and almonds in the aft. But not too much or hell comes back.

The anorexic is so ultra-sensitive that the routine saves her life but break it and it's only strife.

Anti-depressants only increase the hellish nature of life. It's terrifying getting off those things, aye.

The mature anorexic is a saint to live. No alcohol, pot, jet pills, drugs, coffee or caffeine: ick.

ROUTINE TRANSGRESSION

Any transgression of her routine will bring terror. Her bad days becoming mature are bummers.

THE MATURE ANOREXIC

She finds ONE food that works for her and sticks to that. Mine was tacos and raisins in the aft.

Shopping list and nothing other: tortillas, tomatoes, lettuce, cheese, raisins, olives and peppers.

Spaghetti with raw salsa sometimes but it brings weird over-fullness, it just isn't the same, aye.

Having grown up in Southern California it was tacos for me. Others may choose other foods see.

The mature anorexic makes wise decision for herself and her detractors can just go to hell.

OUR FIRST FOOD ADAPTATIONS

Paleo scientists say it's our first food-adaptations that are best for us. Tacos were it, they're delicious.

I had adapted to corn, not to wheat. That's why spaghetti was inferior for this individual see.

The mature anorexic learns isolation is her friend and not to trust many or get hurt again and again.

On the road to maturity she gets hurt by her own pure naiveté: that is, trusting people too early.

MATURITY IS BALANCE

The mature anorexic strikes a balance. 95 on the scales is joyous but lower and it's just too much.

If I weren't a scientist with a Ph.D. they'd lock me up for talking like this as dangerous or at least silly.

I believe E.D. clinics are dangerous. Making them eat thrice a day enforced by dominant lunatics.

28

THE MATURE ANOREXIC

The anorexic is an overachiever and independent. The E.D. clinic makes her cow-tow, it's sad friends.

I was banned from all eating disorder groups on facebook. That's how they are: schmucks.

They want em rounded & curvaceous but the anorexic knows only thin is elegant & advantageous.

THE FALLACY OF E.D. CLINICS

E.D. clinics run on what they "think" not what they know. They are dangerous, let ME tell them how.

They tell the girls how to get used to fullness or see it as a delight. This is so foolish and just not right.

Great actresses in history were thin as could be. Look at Barbara Stanwyck or other greats, see?

Thin is fun, thin feels good. But skip lunch and dinner and they'll look you up, so misunderstood.

Satisfied but empty: starry nights and days are happy. Full and lethargic: it's hell on earth honey.

TO ANOREXICS, A SPECIAL CLASS:

I'm a mature anorexic, finally allowed to be. But I'm established and independent so can be free.

But what of young girls who are locked up and force fed? It's disgusting, I'll say it to the end.

After a history of binging & purging an anorexic is likely to have MCS: multiple chemical sensitivities.

With MCS, everything makes her sick. If smart she'll drop caffeine, alcohol, pot and chocolate.

THE MATURE ANOREXIC

Eat once then by fasting you can handle everything. Eat more than you can't, a bad mood's in swing.

Most people have several undigested meals in their gut along with retained feces making em nuts.

TO FAT COUNSELORS IN ED CLINICS

Many of these are counselors in E.D. clinics, coaching poor anorexics to be like them: lunatics!

It feels so uncomfortable to be in that state. I'm telling you, having break-fast only is the only way.

Spaghetti for my meal won't work for me but it may for you. It all depends what you began with Sue.

A lot of em have potato chips, doesn't seem like much. But that kinda thing lines the cells a bunch.

Let your snacks be raisins/almonds or grapes. You'll be thanking me if that's all you eat later ok.

TAKE THIS ADVICE AND BE HAPPY

To the anorexic: take my advice and you'll be happy. Don't and you'll be victimized badly sweetie.

It was a life-saving revelation I had one day: that full phobia explained all my bad moods ok.

This was such a revelation & discovery my life changed completely and now every day is happy.

As anorexics we are different, a special class. We are achievers & saints but never knew it, alas.

Full-phobia defines us as a class or syndrome. It's not an illness except for the immature & young.

THE MATURE ANOREXIC

The solution for us peculiar ones is to fast every day. The saints fast daily and then give to humanity.

If I die soon it won't be from anorexia. Most do you know, it's the biggest killer for all of ya.

Never force deadlines on yourself for unplanned detours are God's way to improve it all.

MIDLIFE REALIZATIONS

PTSD: NAÏVE CIRCUMSTANCES
INVERTED SYSTEMS
REBELLIOUS CHILDREN
YOUR TIME WILL COME
SYSTEMS THEORY
THE SYSTEM IS LIKE GLUE
THE MATRIX IS BROKEN
IT TAKES A LIFE TO WAKE UP
TRANSCENDING APPROVAL
AUSTERITY HAS GREAT REWARDS

MIDLIFE REALIZATIONS

PTSD: NAÏVE CIRCUMSTANCES

Naive women who get into horrible circumstances end up with PTSD in their old age sis.

If not heeding mom and dad you end up entwined with evil men and it takes a life to recover friend.

We make big mistakes when young and have those evil memories to hold us back when old, huh?

It's like the first half of life is experimenting with things and the second half is getting over it see.

We do things that are culturally acceptable but evil, then suffer later in our own kind of hell.

If evil things are culturally acceptable, chances are mom & dad never condemned them you know.

Sexual energy being so powerful, evil spirits attack making us sick, ugly, pliable and vulnerable.

INVERTED SYSTEMS

All your haughty enemies are now homeless or distressed while you're high up/at your best.

Your foes slammed your name & pinned despicable things on you so now by God they're screwed.

No one treats God's chosen like that and gets away with it. The Psalms repeats that fact, believe it.

Life changes suddenly, losing everything you have. The solution is to be godly, or face these facts.

MIDLIFE REALIZATIONS

Your persecutors are poor, maimed or dead while you're the best in a nice home on a hill instead.

Why have PTSD for everything they did to thee? Look at your gains while they're in a ditch/unfree.

Screaming women and weak men: that's what we see all around and thus we're ruled by evil children.

College rebellion is the result of an immature heart created by liberal parents for the most part.

REBELLIOUS CHILDREN

Rebellious children wanting to protest just look for a good cause. Think of it: isn't it ridiculous?

Our doom: Kill the child in the womb and if he survives let the culture raise him [it's like a bomb].

It's easier for them to put a kid on a drug than to turn off his cell phone so we're all going down, yuk.

At the bottom of all of it is a rejection of God. They don't want a mighty sovereign that's all.

They don't wanna God who draws lines and shows punishments. They want what they wants.

When it comes to relationships, test the waters and don't dive in too quick cuz people are sick.

YOUR TIME WILL COME

Don't your worry, God sees the work you do in private. He rewards you too, just you wait a minute.

He sees your labor when friends say you won't make it or it's irrelevant. Don't worry, He'll reward it.

MIDLIFE REALIZATIONS

Success doesn't come from east or west but from the Lord who puts them down and you as best.

He sees your diligence and orderly ways. No one else sees it but so what, they'll see work pays.

Just keep working and waiting, your ship will eventually come in. It's a promise from God your Friend.

Work hard but then enjoy your day. A true genius has a capacity for leisure not compulsive work ok.

Coming to God is like you found out who your real father is & He happens to own the whole universe.

If you love God, your Father, He will protect you--not those who couldn't care less or eschew.

SYSTEMS THEORY

We're born free [alone] then hooked to an intricate web of competition/envy from those we know.

We're now part of a SYSTEM of rules, regulations and boundaries: curbed by enemies and fools.

We can't be ourselves suddenly. We have to be what others want us to be until we wake up see.

Fears, guilts and shames are inlaid, curbing our behavior, reality and goals until middle aged.

Born free and clear, we enter a system that awaits us and some are kind, some are hateful sis.

The system matrix spreads to the extended family and how we are viewed includes new kids too.

THE SYSTEM IS LIKE GLUE

MIDLIFE REALIZATIONS

How we are viewed is like glue until we don't care anymore. Unfortunately, that's age fifty or more.

Paradoxically, it's when such families break up that most hurt occurs: we were screwed up.

The family breaks up and we crack up. The system was our only reality so now we're messed up.

A healthy system encourages breadth in our reality but a sick one shuts us down to all else see.

We're so busy trying to figure out mixed signals that everything else is off limits/goes to hell.

Through no fault of our own dad has an affair. Mom is nuts & the system breaks down from there.

Mixed signals, contradictions, mean comparisons: the result of the sick system is **EXHAUSTION**.

Even after we're gone the system carries on. In our middle age the same games split us hon'.

Even when we're old we feel left out in the cold. Finding things to calm our nerves/make us bold.

The script was encoded in the brain early and that's all we have to deal with until/without therapy.

Dad has an affair then mom starts drinking. The kids try it too then one is killed when out partying.

THE MATRIX IS BROKEN

The cherished matrix was broken and our entire reality was forsaken. A happy childhood, forgotten.

When angry at mom, dad calls the daughter fat. She becomes bulimic to deal with stress: fact.

MIDLIFE REALIZATIONS

The system is nonsummative. All parts fit together & the whole transcends the parts, it's relative.

What about when a step-family is grafted in. Now the real hell begins with mean comparisons.

The new families are trashed when the Christian ethic was bashed. Sin set in: it all turned to ash.

Your mean sister uses you new step son as a wedge against you, not caring you are dying Sue.

You're so screwed up you go to your old childhood home and they call the cops, you're on your own.

You move to a new town carrying this shit around and they gossip/call you crazy and it's profound.

At 40 you need father and mother but they're long gone forever and you're still a child my brother.

When you finally hit bottom you say "Yes God, change my life" and you start again, free of strife.

IT TAKES A LIFE TO WAKE UP

With your heavenly father at the helm the old system is smashed in your head & your newly owned.

It's scary at first, you're so used to the emotional thirst. Daily renewal of God's focus puts Him first.

Happiness may not come before latter years: when all the stingers stop from older women/peers.

Not until I had my own home, relocated/owned, was I free of mixed signals & cruel contradictions of society.

Not til I had my own [relocated] home was I free of mixed signals & contradictions of society.

MIDLIFE REALIZATIONS

Not til I was done with all addictions including prescribed pot was I truly free of the rot.

Then I had to deal with all the stuff I had smoked down: a lifetime of suffering with people around.

They didn't understand me, they persecuted & snubbed me. I had to overcome the resulting PTSD.

TRANSCENDING APPROVAL

They used me and I let em do it: anything for approval, another obstruction--you'd better believe it.

This all took a lifetime but hopefully not for you. Read my words/grow up early to enjoy life in lieu.

It took a life to recognize my chemical sensitivities. Until then I was always sick/laid up see.

It took a life to recognize I needed rest. That avoiding/isolating from people stress is best.

Some people--God's chosen--are meant to be alone. They're to stand out and stay on their throne.

Don't let men use you cuz they'll always try to do it. I had to learn the art: saying "NO" to all of it.

I had to learn the art of marriage and adapting to that took years too--you bet it does Sue.

I had to learn how to live and dress without trying so hard to impress. Humility without stress.

I had to learn to stop picking bones with people. If they wanna be a dam liberal, just you avoid evil.

The choices we make in life often twist our path beyond our control. It's real important to avoid evil.

MIDLIFE REALIZATIONS

People you lost whom you'll never see again. Lost to eternity and swallowed up in sin.

AUSTERITY HAS GREAT REWARDS

Austerity has great rewards. Fasting expands time while eating/other pleasures makes one old, aye.

Anyone can eat/drink for momentary pleasure but you miss the moment/synchronicities for sure.

While fasting I'm in an Italian villa with ancient thoughts but in eating it's just mundanity I bought.

Drinking doesn't expand time, you only want more. It's external, not giving you eternity to explore.

I've been into all of it: eating, drinking and going to restaurants. Fasting taught me the opposite.

What seems like it opens only closes you down. With self-deprivation you explore new grounds.

Eat your delicious tacos in morning then fast all day: busy in your doings as time extends to eternity.

Eat then clean the kitchen and don't go in there again. You've got more important things my friend.

You will be so happy living this way. Who ever heard of fasting by starting with a feast each day?

THEY PINNED SIN ON YOU

THEY PINNED SINS ON YOU
THE CORRUPT SPEAK LOFTILY
THE WHOLE GROUP HATES YOU
TURN IT ALL AROUND
THEY CREATE MENTAL ILLNESS
WATCH OUT FOR "NICE"
ON FALSE RELIGIONS
YOUR SO-CALLED FRIENDS
ONE MEAL A DAY *IS* FASTING

THEY PINNED SIN ON YOU

Those who love Jesus do it from gratitude: that their sins are wiped away--they're clean dude.

The unhappiest people I know are those surprised that life isn't fair. Wake up, have joy and be rare.

Success depends on how well you handle plan B. You gotta keep going, no matter how bad it seems.

But loss is not loss, pain is not pain--but for us choosing it again, and again and again ok.

THEY PINNED SINS ON YOU

The evil pin corrupt sins on the believer. But he's been forgiven while they go down to hell quicker.

It's a horrible day when you see all that was imputed to thee but no worries, God is your Daddy.

Your accusers are heady with power til that blessed hour when He turns on them like a shower.

Suddenly you see it all: how it fits together how they persecuted you, those birds of a feather.

It was THEM with dirty minds but they put it all on you in a giant projection from the filthy/unkind.

To overcome this giant projection by the non-election you must know you are forgiven, amen.

THE CORRUPT SPEAK LOFTILY

The corrupt speak loftily like you're the guilty but God'll take em down swiftly: they are dead see.

THEY PINNED SIN ON YOU

Where are your persecutors? They cannot be found. You search for them but they're in the ground.

The evil are arrogant. That's their main characteristic but have no fear, now you can have merriment.

THE WHOLE GROUP HATES YOU

Due to social hypnotism and envy the whole town hates you. That's how it works in the human zoo.

It's embarrassing to wake up to all they pinned on you, a projection from filthy minds and untrue.

These are the ungodly who prosper in the world and increase in riches, putting you in ditches.

If you didn't know God, this massive projection could have triggered mental illness, but it did not.

The fast is such a sudden change it brought up these realizations but hold on for your reward hon'.

All day long you're been plagued and chastened every morning when they were the guilty things.

What causes mental illness? Other people. See this or take it on thinking you're the one who is evil.

TURN IT ALL AROUND

Turn it around! Your accusers were the unsound having to put all the blame on you, God's own.

They hate you [the chosen] the minute they see you then get wind of gossip & it's a sealed deal.

It's the canyon before success. We all go through this test of our strength in the human mess.

THEY PINNED SIN ON YOU

We're all sinners & our ugliness shows here. The crowd is a bully when it comes to this dear.

You grew old and your beauty withered in the face of your persecutors but God was your savior.

I've written 98 books on this: persecution of the evil crowd against the Elect and the blameless.

THEY CREATE MENTAL ILLNESS

Not seeing this matrix can lead one into mental illness. Feeling shame like there's hopeless evil in us.

It starts with the scapegoating family then carries on to new systems that get wind of it see.

You think it's never going to end but God is your friend and He inverts the whole system, amen!

You put up with it for years so now God will reward giving you back tenfold for all your tears.

To the adulterer: go and sin no more, for who are your accusers? Those who went to the whores.

Should we pray for success or repentance? Put the onus where it should be then God grants it.

What would I do if I didn't have you to talk to about the contradictions in the human zoo?

WATCH OUT FOR "NICE"

The whole problem is they're so "nice". But you feel mentally ill inside cuz evil is subtle, aye.

Contradictions: You walk away feeling to blame, like you're the one who's racist, evil or lame.

THEY PINNED SIN ON YOU

The worst wife-batterers are very "nice". Evil must always have another side to cover up its vice.

The "nice but evil" are so subtle you think you had a nice conversation but later you're befuddled.

The falsest religions are seen as "good people". But Jesus said only God is good/the rest are evil.

ON FALSE RELIGIONS

False religions stress the importance of family but the bible says our worst enemies are in it ok.

Everything is in reverse from what you think/have been taught. It's amazing all the lies we bought.

Watch out for nice and feel comfortable with just normal. The latter is rare & nice is immoral.

The nice are very popular but that's the devil's crowd. The godly are usually alone and not so loud.

How could the nice leave you depressed? That's the question: you should see it as a giant test.

Fast from dawn to dusk. Eat a regular meal for breakfast then at dusk eat grapes or cantaloupe last.

In dense generations women or children rule. Things degrade and the men are regarded as fools.

YOUR SO-CALLED FRIENDS

Did your so-called friend take advantage when you were down by spreading it all around?

The faith that triumphs over challenges is the same that moves mountains and divides seas sis.

THEY PINNED SIN ON YOU

Suffering produces perseverance then character then hope w/out shame cuz we know God ok.

"Mourning Becomes Electra": best example of systems theory where patterns never change see.

"Electra" was a Greek tragedy where family patterns repeat and repeat until they're dead see.

The repetitions are uncanny.   The patterns would be funny if they weren't so tragic in their endings.

Try Therapeutic Playwriting: write a play about the repetitions in your own dysfunctional family.

ONE MEAL A DAY *IS* FASTING

This IS fasting, as odd as it seems: to have a huge breakfast then fast the rest of the day see.

This IS fasting, no matter what they say: Eat four guacamole tacos then fast the rest of today.

THE OLD IS BEST

Since the narcissist loves you at first but discards you later, narc abuse is a very painful matter.

Neurotics have a Low C Factor: the inability to learn from their mistakes, it all just repeats.

The main characteristic of addiction is anosognosia: the inability to see your own condition.

To the blind I hope to open up their psych to a brand new wonderful world beyond the hype.

The more we delete the more we attract. It's called pneumaticity: making a space for it.

There's an evil army all around but God will snatch you outa the throng and give you a new home.

THE THING ABOUT HUMANS

Here's the thing: human nature is shit. Conservatives defend against it but liberals give into it.

Liberals allow/cave into the lowest drives of mankind: promiscuous sex and baby killing.

After abusing God's daughter God took his two kids and made the third one a whoremonger.

Best plan for older women: get headlines at night from the best but spend days in PC rest.

One day he seems victorious but the next he's mowed down or shown as foolish, just you watch.

THE OLD IS BEST

Never chase a man just cuz it's easy on your PC. It's still inferior and not the way it is to be.

We like being together but like solitude better so it's two in separate cornucopia on 3 acres.

Go into their house, you're the victim of the cumulative chemicals from all their belongings.

People have so much ambivalency and/or opportunity that you're not number one and feel it see.

The jerk forces you in petty competition with other women in his domain, putting you in shame.

HARDLY NUMBER ONE

You're hardly number one with this man, he's gotta whole stable and for you it means bedlam.

This never happens to the queen. She knows instantly when competing to be noticed/seen.

She's way up here and little man is down there forcing her to compete with his cheerleaders.

Get outa his matrix immediately. He's not gonna change and it's a dam losing game honey.

If you were filthy rich would you put up with this: recurrently being sadistically bewitched?

He's putting you in competition with lesser but younger women and you feel down: duh.

Get outa this matrix or you're dead. You can't settle for less unless you want depression instead.

I've been in this situation and it's horrible. Never stand for a man like that: it's totally unstable.

THE OLD IS BEST

Turn it around. What would he do if you triangulated with other men? Think on this woman.

Every time you think of this immature hustler recall all the crap in the war until mentally it's over.

Never compete with other women cuz it's always petty and them putting you down [calumny].

PETTY COMPETITIONS

Instead of pettily competing with a witch, quietly remove yourself from an impossible matrix.

She's putting you down behind the scenes: there's a Jezebel complex in all women in seems.

She's dissuading him from liking you and she's chasing him too: good, it shows she's inferior Sue.

Don't waste your life cuz it goes really fast. If smart you can maximize each day/have a blast.

FOX sided with the old bags from The View. Thank God Laura, Hannity and Waters are left too.

Jealousy: you want his toy. Envy: You don't want him to have it either--this drives human history.

Genius brings left and right together: sees the seriousness of problem but knows God is higher.

Him stealing things was the fork in the road I needed cuz there's no going back lest unheeded.

If you know God exists then do you realize His punishments come thru people attacks?

MENTAL ILLNESS AND CHEMICALS

THE OLD IS BEST

Most illness is chemical accumulation from your own belongings. Eliminate or get moving.

I had to eliminate my belongings or move out to a cottage in the back and instantly got well.

You got too much stuff: chemical contamination overloading immunity makes life very rough.

The cottage was humble, small and totally pure. I could breathe again, I thanked the Lord.

Depending on the weather I either smell sawdust or dander but in my straw house I'm ok dear.

LIBERALS: ABORTION UP TO BIRTH!

The liberals want abortion up to birth and even baby execution after it: what an evil scourge.

The collective IQ of "The View" is around 85 so I am never surprised by their silly diatribes.

Does a female athlete have to get her neck broken by a male to finally see leftist insanity as a fail?

FOX lost two billion dollars in 72 hours and still think it was right to kick Tucker out the door.

The left is very good at organizing people against media personalities: always treachery.

Tucker flipped a light in the dark so we could see the cockroaches and it's beautiful--know it.

Carlson is a mere archetype of us all. Great victory finally is at hand tho' it seems like the end.

Fox fired Tucker to maintain semi lobotomized quasi retarded population. Army Psyop Expert

THE OLD IS BEST

So a message of tranquility and prosperity is now called being a "violence seeker"? Insanity.

The population isn't exactly lobotomized but in a trance, daydream or spell: drought = mental.

Ratings show that since they fired Tucker people are rejecting ALL cable news as a bummer.

I can see that, I'm sick of it too. I don't watch The Five anymore, it's all lost fidelity/amplitude.

Even Hannity lost a million viewers. That's what I mean--we're sick of the entire media scene.

Our destiny is all planned. God has the future: He created it, no need to do it, just fall into it.

RESTORE OLD PATHS

FALSE ACCUSATION
EVERY WOMAN IS A QUEEN
PURPOSE FIRST
SINGLE CELIBATES & ECCENTRICS
IDENTITY PRECEDES RELATIONSHIP
OLDER IS THE CROWN OF LIFE
OBSESSING OVER RELATIONSHIPS
HEAL BEFORE RELATIONSHIP
EARLY TRAUMA INFLUENCES
IMPROVE YOUR LEGACY FIRST
CHEAP SLUTS WITH HIGH DEGREES
CRUEL BEASTS AND THE PHILISTINES
TRAUMA BONDS
CALUMNY: SOUL MURDER BY SISTER
TRIANGULATION FRUSTRATION
WOMEN CAN BE DANGEROUS
EXPECT NO PITY FROM THESE PEOPLE
REAL RELATIONSHIPS
FOLLOW THESE RULES
YOUTH PROTESTS
HIGHEST BORDERS POSSIBLE
THEY MOVE TO COMFY NEIGHBORHOODS
LIBERALISM ENDS IN DECAY
OUR SOLACE IS OUR HOME
THE MALE FEMINIST IS A SADIST
A REAL MAN VS. FEMINISTS
WHITE NATIONALISM
WE'RE HERDED INTO GROOVES
THE LEFT'S "HELP" IS TO CONTROL

RESTORE OLD PATHS

THE COMMUNIST SPIRIT
MENTAL DROUGHTS & SENSUAL THOUGHTS
FAKE CHURCHES
PREACH HELL/HEAVEN, SIN/REPENTANCE
THE LEFT PLAYS DIRTY POLITIX
THE MARVELOUS WORK AND WONDER
DON'T BEMOAN PAST MISTAKES
WHEN YOU HAVE BUT PTSD TRASHES IT
YOU DON'T JUST GET THE PERSON
HOME RULES NOT TAUGHT IN SCHOOLS
HOLY SPIRIT EASE: GOD SMOOTHES THINGS OUT
LIFE WILL ACTUALLY BE EASY
"THEY'RE ALL GOOD" IS MALICIOUS FALSEHOOD
GOD TAKES THE PRESSURE OFF
IT'S A NEW DAY, HURRAY!
WOMEN FEEL SORRY
FREAKS: YOUR KID'S GUESTS ARE SICK
THESE PEOPLE ARE NOT YOUR FRIENDS
GOD ALWAYS GIVES YOU ESCAPE
EVIL FREAKS: BEYOND GROSS
YOUR TORMENTERS ARE OLD MEN NOW
LIBERALISM IS CAPTURED BY PROJECTIONS
GROWING MUSCLE FROM RESISTANCE
IMMUNITY IS IN THE GUT
EAT CALORICALLY DENSE ONCE A DAY
GET SOME CLASS IN THE KITCHEN: CHANGE SPOONS
AUTOIMMUNE RESPONSES ARE AN ATTACK
PRESSURES OF AUTOIMMUNITY

RESTORE OLD PATHS

FALSE ACCUSATION

False accusation is torture and little can change it, even relocation won't erase inner shame son.

It was easy for her to do it, I was an easy target being strange & novel to them right off the bat.

She took advantage of that. She could pass go and I could not: people love to hate the odd girl out.

Bullying is a growing epidemic. One third of American students say they've been bullied, bad.

Victims of bullying are 9 x more likely to commit suicide. False accusation and division into sides.

EVERY WOMAN IS A QUEEN

"Every woman is a queen" means: they have far greater value than the world has given them see.

The bible talks of God's people taking dominion. That's all the king and queen concept means.

The queen message resonates with rural, urban, young, old, parochial or around the world: go girl.

Queens don't obsess over relationships, they work on certain things while they wait for their mate.

God didn't create you obsessed with relationship. You have work to do not be down in the pits.

It's a matter of you having a purpose, something unique--a talent put in you even before your birth.

RESTORE OLD PATHS

A man using you for sex or money obliterates that purpose and makes you sick inside miss.

PURPOSE FIRST

God gave you purpose before you ever came into relationship: it predates and determines it.

Purpose first: In the process of fulfilling it you come into union with people called relationship.

In good relationships you soar: People who are suitable for the purpose you came into the earth for.

Marriage is the merger of two people with similar purpose. We're not born just for relationship sis.

It's ok to desire relationship [it's necessary for kingdom dominion] but it should not come first.

SINGLE CELIBATES & ECCENTRICS

Like Paul, many are content being single. They're called "eccentrics" and they live a lot longer too.

It's society putting a weird image on you for not having a mate or even supposing you are gay ok.

Many of my ancestors were single, celibate and childless: busy churchgoers and productive.

Married men are healthier and happier than single ones, that's a statistical fact: marriage is great.

Once you've identified your God-given purpose NOW you can figure out who accommodates it.

God made Adam first. He put Adam to sleep. He creates Eve who He brings to Adam for union see.

IDENTITY PRECEDES RELATIONSHIP

RESTORE OLD PATHS

Recap: each had identity in themselves before coming together. Individuals before couple sir.

The problem is finding in coupling what they shoulda discovered in their individuality initially.

We see divorces and huge dyssynchronies because people did not master individuality first see.

Once God is done with something it's over and no one even remembers it: it's hard but believe it.

Just as you flip a switch from negative to positive God makes you white as snow after repentance.

OLDER IS THE CROWN OF LIFE

The problem with older is you've more history to remorse over yet it's the best phase ever.

The reason I have ten times more energy than a youngster is I'm a sober faster pot lover.

I eat once a day if that, stay away from brats and listen to music looking at the view with tokes.

The reason I have ten times more energy than youngsters is I'm a sober fasting pot lover.

Smear campaigns are cruel cuz people hear something and tuck it away as truth for filing.

False accusations are horrible and I've felt it all my life. There's nothing you can say but pray, aye.

Hang on to pastor, not that crystal lady. Separate pagans from reality and guides to eternity.

A queen concentrates on things she controls and leaves things that aren't up to God that's all.

RESTORE OLD PATHS

A relationship is never completely under your control. The best you can do is your part that's all.

By obsessing on relationships the things she can control fade along with the divine attractions too.

We must develop as an individual so he who's ordained as a partner will readily recognize us too.

Adam recognized Eve as the female version of himself as Eve completed her development.

OBSESSING OVER RELATIONSHIPS

When obsessing over relationship not purpose we fail to develop into selfhood, the attraction magnet.

Thus when the person ordained for you shows up they will be able to recognize you/your stuff.

Thus when the person ordained for you shows up they will be able to recognize/call you "woman".

The queen is not obsessing over "him" but busy about her purpose, vision, goals and ambitions.

Ask: Have you completed your personal growth? Are you where you should be on your path?

If not there are things you should be working on while waiting for your mate: credit rate, educate.

Complete the things God has given you to do then you can take pride in yourself alone too.

Number one is YOUR personal growth so that self-confidence becomes strong, even bold.

HEAL BEFORE RELATIONSHIP

RESTORE OLD PATHS

If you've had childhood trauma, don't you think you should solve that before another suffers?

The obsessor isn't even healthy enough to entertain thoughts of a relationship but she does it.

You still have soul ties from a past, you're still crying or broken from a father wound, you're crass.

Broken over a missing father you desperately want a man to fill that painful hole there.

EARLY TRAUMA INFLUENCES

You could be using this present man to solve a tie to a previous one who's still in your soul/brain.

Do you love God? Be obsessed with His things and you won't have room for obsessing desiring.

She that is unmarried cares for the things of the Lord. Not obsessing over a man or being alone.

Where there is no vision the people perish. If you don't recognize it how can he a confused mess?

Even if finding the perfect man you sabotage it from not perfecting self before the marriage began.

You are fulfilled from expressing the vision in your heart not from marriage but that's the best start.

Much of her inner pain had come from not fulfilling her inner purpose not from his indifference.

IMPROVE YOUR LEGACY FIRST

Do you need to be remembered? A queen works on her legacy while waiting for her mate for sure.

RESTORE OLD PATHS

You won't be remembered for your mate but what you accomplished here by your death date.

If obsessing over relationship you're not doing anything to be remembered for, just a sunken ship.

Relationship is not accomplishment. You must find out why you're here and do that then marry him.

You still have to leave a legacy even if married. You must develop before and after union see.

I pray that the spirit of God will cause you to know who you are in Him and that your mate comes in.

I pray you rise above low standards the world has for you, that you're a woman of substance too.

Live with purpose every single day to maximize what God has put uniquely into your life, aye!

It's Friday. Turn it all off and go into timeless space and the right-brain with evocative music, hurray.

CHEAP SLUTS WITH HIGH DEGREES

Modern women don't want commitment and are promiscuous. Abused, PTSD persists.

So she's a cheap slut with a Ph.D. or lawyer's degree. She's still abused cuz it's a spiritual thing.

Time and the generations pass and all you're worried about dissolves as a vapor/as if never.

Since women superior in education/income are abused and get PTSD they must vet carefully.

CRUEL BEASTS AND THE PHILISTINES

These are cruel beasts, also known as the philistines. Impervious to beauty, cruel, dastardly.

They remind me of a dark cavern. Wolves ready to collude together and eat one up as victim.

Of course they bring friends, that's how weak they feel in your presence, don't let em in.

Sex is the one last arena men even the score cuz now women are better educated/make more.

Evening the score cuz you make more: Now abused she's gotta deal with PTSD and mourn.

Something is wrong and it's not her education or high income it's her immorality, that's it hon'

Get your head outa the dungeon they put you in with all their petty disparagins' and put downs.

Realize all the dam implications of this sister abuse thing and how it impacted medically.

Sibling abuse is hidden--behind closed doors and covered up by others the narc adores.

TRAUMA BONDS

These toxic ties were trauma bonds. Picture yourself cutting em then feeling the exhilaration.

Visualize yourself cutting ties then feeling free. Walks on the beach, no more fearing the beastly.

How can you get back at someone who's dead? Eventually we have to just forgive instead.

Blame shifting: Have they simply dumped it all onto you? You're the entire problem in this thing.

Typically a scapegoat is not aware people are gossiping about them until many years later on.

RESTORE OLD PATHS

As years go on you finally unravel mysterious pieces of the puzzle and it's shocking/unbelievable.

All of a sudden your eyes are wide open and you understand your downfall: you're appalled.

How your sister slandered you to a stranger in your presence and you totally missed it.

CALUMNY: SOUL MURDER BY SISTER

You now understand why everyone who knew your sister turned against you suddenly, what monsters.

Being in that family was like being chained to a tree as they kept hitting me and I couldn't get free.

I suddenly saw how mom triangulated every single relationship I had behind my back: so bad.

Sister abuse shows the worst characteristics of Jezebel and there's no escape--it's just criminal.

Everything the narc does is underhanded and the monkeys completely go along with it.

There is so much hate, envy, bitterness and discord as he invites hundreds of monkeys to the war.

The victim can't reveal the screw-job cuz they'll turn the screws tighter and she's still tied there.

It could be your ex-spouse's friends all ganging up on you. It's horrifying what monkeys do.

"Hey you're gaslighting/triangulating me and ruining all my relationships!" Instead I was speechless.

They can easily deny it since it's all of them against you, proving the problem is you, a shrew.

RESTORE OLD PATHS

Crazy-making happens with blame-shifting in these unhealthy relationship dynamics: lunatics.

First you're in control then suddenly you're to blame for it all: the environment is beyond hostile.

TRIANGULATION FRUSTRATION

Triangulation is when the narcissist brings a third party into the relationship to maintain control.

Triangulation is like a leaking boat, a loose canon, an attempt to herd cats, betrayal/chaos.

You talk to somebody and the narcissist gets to them next and dissuades them the other way.

Female power games are always social: networking, gossiping and calumny on the phone.

Narc is the ring leader playing people against each other while always appearing innocent sir.

The narc's army is the thing here. Due to weakness they will employ MANY flying monkeys for war.

Jezebel would always bring a male friend to come against me but I didn't realize it then.

Women inciting riots on targets hurt or maimed for life. Tell me women aren't dangerous, yikes!

WOMEN CAN BE DANGEROUS

Women in power condemning whole classes to longer prison sentences or letting out criminals.

Powerful aunts/mothers colluding with lawyers/psychiatrists to punish the scapegoat fast.

RESTORE OLD PATHS

Tell me women aren't dangerous, especially when irrational panic thinking is added to this.

Making decisions based on what their neighbor's say or what was said on The View today: not ok.

Women are manipulated by "he said this about you" and thus triggered out comes the shrew.

A normal person would check truth of rumor but a low-minded monkey never checks the facts sir.

The narcissist's monkey army are dumbed, suggestible and biting at the bit to do his dirty work quick.

A flying monkey doesn't check for facts, honesty, integrity--he only fulfills a shared fantasy.

They never check for authenticity or transparency, it's just what the narc says about it see.

EXPECT NO PITY FROM THESE PEOPLE

Expect no pity from these people. They are predators when strangers, rely on God nothing evil.

Don't expect the kindness of strangers and you won't get hurt. Pull yourself up/put God first.

Expect nothing and you won't be disappointed again. That's maturity vs. the entitled generation.

It's scary as hell what we've been thru but God wants to sweeten our minds and memories too.

What we're up against: Insecure, uneducated people without common sense & easily brainwashed.

Brainwashed by whoever's in power in family or has money, not meritocracy or moral decency.

RESTORE OLD PATHS

So the empath sees the slide to the side of the snide and feels powerless, unworthy, despised.

REAL RELATIONSHIPS

Modern dates are glorified hookups in today's sad world. We should want intimacy not this girls.

Critical in relationships is willingness to be vulnerable to pain and hurt, can you do this?

You're in a real relationship [not fantasy realm] if you have goals and are working towards them.

Real relationships show strengths/weaknesses but in fantasy bonds one is devalued or idealized.

Micro-relationships [hookups] lead nowhere except to depression, anxiety and substance abuse.

They end in heartbreak or sexual assault. PTSD, horrible memories--is this what you want?

Loss of autonomy and agency. Coming under others due to shame see-- becoming weaselly.

FOLLOW THESE RULES

Shared narcissistic fantasies block your destiny. Make sure you're in a real relationship, be happy.

You should never merge or fuse with your partner. Maintain true selfhood always and forever.

World doesn't care about you so think before you act. Strangers are not kind, life can turn black.

Follow these rules. Treat yourself with dignity and don't allow anyone to disrespect you.

RESTORE OLD PATHS

Make clear boundaries and make known to others what is acceptable and what is out of bounds.

Do not tolerate aggression in any form whether girls or guys. Instantly terminate unequivocally.

Be assertive/explicit about your needs and expectations from others. Do not be arrogant but firm.

I will treat others as I want them to treat me and lead by way of example maintaining my well being.

Zero tolerance for boundary busters/abusers cuz I've learned my lesson about self-preservation.

Happiness is from the inside. Do not confuse with gratification from the outside: opposites.

Nothing is more sad and lonely than casual sex in order to feel less sad and lonely. Sam Vaknin

Self-discipline, diligence, tenacity of a bull dog. Lotsa competition but no worries/we've got God@

RESTORE OLD PATHS

WHO is doing this? It's the YOUTH who've been told to hate America in the public schools, it's "cool".

YOUTH PROTESTS

They're all youth who are doing this! It helps to see this as a war and the division [who's agreeing with this?]

RESTORE OLD PATHS

WHO is justifying this mass mayhem? Nail it down--there's never an excuse-- but these are your friends?

As the years pass you won't be a king for long so be a king now and give it your best, entirely triumphant.

Blacks are 12% of the population but black on white crime is ten times higher than white on black, amen.

It's not that our liberal friends are ignorant but that they know so much that is not so. Mr. Reagan

Even in the sixties this wouldn't have happened. How far we have fallen, need a MORAL revolution.

WHY does this shock you when the youth have been trained to hate America for decades too?

A sign of low intelligence is minimizing things of major importance or making a big deal outa nothing.

Trump needs to decapitate Antifa today with a high profile FBI arrest and the national guard in all states.

Crowd control and RIOT control are two completely different things. Kick it up a notch, please!

Three groups: 1] legit protestors, 2] Antifa mobsters and then 3] LOOTERS [criminal opportunists].

STOP SAYING WHITES ARE BAD

While white schools taught us not to hate but to love they also said the white man was very, VERY bad.

The message in our schools was very simple: dark men are good but white people are BAD and very evil.

"But blacks are the victims so how could they ever be racist?" This is the GIST of liberal madness.

RESTORE OLD PATHS

This is the result of a leftist media and school system brainwashing Americans for decades now.

It all comes down to this: there's a group of people who want to destroy America and they go to all events.

They need a political MOMENT to posture but in reality they're just stealing and destroying culture.

"Yes there are leftists there but there are also white supremacist groups"-- shut up you liar.

It got violent cuz the youth ARE violent and have been since the 70's-80's feeling entitled as always.

They travel across state lines using military style tactics to destroy everything: this is WAR, believe it.

America's campaign against racism turned it into one of the most racist places in the world against white men.

BJs ? "I'm not a fan, it makes me gag/throw up. My husband likes it but I gotta be drunk." -lady

We're in a war with organized violent radicals who go from town to town fully supported by the liberals.

The glories of Europe came from nationalism: charming cultures not forced and cruel homogeneity, torture.

Part of PTSD recovery is reliving toxic memories tho' we try not to. See the system then you're through.

HIGHEST BORDERS POSSIBLE

We fight for what Christians have always fought for: to just be left alone!

Tho' in safe circumstances now I'm plagued with memories when I was invaded constantly without a wall.

RESTORE OLD PATHS

They are simply without values, morals or ethics and seem to be proud of it. Nihilistic, grabby, sick.

Lessons I endured to want the **HIGHEST BORDERS POSSIBLE** were horrible but now I'm telling y'all.

It's not enough to lock your home you gotta have a **FENCE** and locked gate or it's still very bad fate.

You don't want them knocking on your door or getting that far! You need a buffer zone and a **WALL**.

They simply want what you have and in light of the communist spirit think they deserve it, called "sharing".

You must **GO LOW** around the communist spirit cuz you can't have what you want without sharing it.

That's why the rich must sequester: As the lowly covets what they have they're magnets for disaster.

The Great White Hope pooh-poohed modern BS and brought us back to common sense/old paths.

Obama put into place laws--"loopholes" setting this up--so now there's nothing we can do about it.

Flooding the border, multitudes each day. There's nothing we can do cuz Obama set it up this way.

I don't wanna be around for the browning of America--it's two different realities and we're losing ours.

Obama wanted to integrate white neighborhoods--they want to move to our towns which are so good.

THEY MOVE TO COMFY NEIGHBORHOODS

They move to our comfortable neighborhoods then hate our guts as they keep to their own and fuss.

RESTORE OLD PATHS

In this multicultural milieu they're called "superior". So they invade our lands seeing us as inferior.

All liberal cities become havens to this far left democratic economic globalist side effect: rich-poor divide.

70's: Things still nice but changing sexually. 80's: Things go liberal triggering 90's hex, now: a wreck.

LIBERALISM ENDS IN DECAY

When a town goes liberal it's really sad. It's like a demon black cloud comes over the whole crowd.

Mrs. Copley left La Casa Del Zorro to obese homosexual son who made it for gays/ran it into the ground.

How fast Borrego Springs changed: from an upper middle class republican town to trees dying all around.

Borrego was charming and clean but now you see trash overflow, trees dying and sexual immorality.

How sad it was when all that old world charm was lost at La Casa Del Zorro in Borrego. Just like em all.

It was clean, crisp manicured neighborhoods now it's a hodgepodge of careless tenants or boys in hoods.

My own neighborhood in La Mesa went from longterm neighbors to transients and people milling around.

When I went back to my home town I cried. The devastating crowdedness, the coldness, the grime.

I just hope I can maintain the delicious sweet privacy in nature I have at this time, for my lifetime.

But they don't want us to have rural life--the prejudice against us cowboys and middle Americans is rife.

RESTORE OLD PATHS

OUR SOLACE IS OUR HOME

My solace is my head and my home. Staying clear for just my own thoughts and enjoying our home alone.

Prediction: Soon we won't be able to say we love our home, since that is being mean to the homeless.

The public is so ill informed that those who've been in there get re-elected from name-recognition alone.

Like all pseudo-intellectuals Cortez distracts through non-issues as one giant SPEED BUMP.

And after completion it's up there for eternity or as long as Amazon will have me.

Never vote for politicians making a career of moral grandstanding.

Poison was injected in sixties and now we see the full-blown horrible, disastrous effects on the country.

Democrats and lefties are preparing tyranny. They're afraid to debate us so disenfranchise us, truly.

I don't mind the hard work but I sure mind the hard waiting. How to speed destiny: eat once daily.

The young twit feminists flew paper airplanes at me cuz I wouldn't use the pronouns they wanted.

The absolute cruelest--least sensitive to female emotions--was the male feminist, a true sadist.

THE MALE FEMINIST IS A SADIST

Liberals see themselves as humane hearty angels but that's just the surface of their horrible shadow.

The male feminist read all the books and knew the jargon. Yet it was all bull--he was the most cruel/no fun.

RESTORE OLD PATHS

He would jerk me around because my viewpoints weren't feminist enough: come-here-go-away stuff.

True sensitivity was when I met a traditional (real) man. He was so considerate I never felt hurt again.

A military career man who was protective and responsible. Not a liberal feminist bore like the rabble.

Male and female fit perfectly/complement each other. Viva la difference--they wanna destroy that forever?

Male feminist goes along with that stuff. He toes the line like a simpleton to deranged values/silly myths.

What a cuckhold--a male feminist, really? He parrots what the women want him to say? That's a loser, truly.

A REAL MAN VS. FEMINISTS

A real man stands up to these crazy feminists: "We don't like you not cuz you're female but as stupid tyrants."

Angry, bitchy, entitled, weird, loud, arrogant as hell, mean, ingrown, narrow: that's the liberal feminist.

They magnify side issues which are really non-issues. AOC makes a big deal outa nothing, the shrew.

The male feminist so concerned about women's issues put me on emotional rollercoasters apres screwed.

Major reason for explosion of male suicide is being raised by feminist mothers as their maleness died.

Radical feminist in her fifties was so dogmatic she'd get violent with me--we are seeing female pugnacity.

She said me sitting with hands folded in lap was WAY too rigid and white, I needed to relax, she tyrannized.

RESTORE OLD PATHS

WHITE NATIONALISM

"Repressive tolerance" is honoring movements from the left and repressing those of the right.

Due to these repressive hearings, American patriots are now to be labeled as "White Nationalists".

They say White Nationalists are purveyors of "hate" when all we want is to be left alone with locked gate.

As the Paradigm of Tolerance moves the Overton window, violence is justified against whites you know.

"Is it ok to hit a white Nazi unprovoked?" Yes I was always taught that was a good thing he joked.

"Some speech requires a more visceral response" he said after he punched the white nationalist.

The Overton Window of "normalcy" just assumes the American Patriot is a Nazi deserving of violence.

This is such a dangerous transformation I predict a white genocidal race war soon and it's the Overton.

The Overton Window: The ideas which are tolerated in public discourse. When it moves it justifies WAR.

Televised mental illness legitimizes attacking free-thinking Americans and is now perfectly acceptable.

They expect us to accept their savvy tongue-and-cheek arrogant hypocrisy as relevant and cute.

They expect us to accept their anti-American far-left extremism and Antifa which to them is self-evident.

Even though I'm a filthy sinner like everyone else, God still supports and will reward my marvelous works.

RESTORE OLD PATHS

The anti-American anti-Trump stronghold-upholders are absolutely despicable and it means friends I know.

WE'RE HERDED INTO GROOVES

They're herded into grooves, that's the way it is. Meanwhile a unique artist is screened out, dismissed.

In DALLAS (1980's) it was all about that--but didn't SHOW that--so it had class.

The dems use of immigrants: Flood red areas to flip em but don't you dare send em to our blue towns.

Now the democrats are seeing mass enrichment as a punishment?

They always called em low crime, productive, tax-paying economic booms but they don't want em soon.

You must see the system: Your sins brought on their bad behavior. It's a relief then it's erased by Savior.

We introject (swallow) the trauma, make a template of the situation then project it again on all we know.

He pays the bills so I can stay afloat in my beautiful home and work all day so I don't ask for more, ok?

The mark of a scientific discovery is: DOES IT WORK? You be the judge, you confirm it.

A male feminist can't think.

Most relationships are NOTHING BUT the blind leading the blind.

They say we're in the "beta cucks" era, post male and female. That's why they hate Trump, an alpha male.

China controls Hollywood's movies: family and country-destroying art is financed by our enemies!

RESTORE OLD PATHS

Pocahontus seems earnest while saying nothing while Trump makes common sense ringing true to me.

THE LEFT'S "HELP" IS TO CONTROL

When the left "helps people" it's always using someone else's money and it's not to aid but for power.

Democrats have controlled blacks for sixty years. Do they have better schools and happy families, or tears?

Liberals put themselves in authority to judge thoughts, feelings and actions of others/ruin their brothers.

It's group acceptance of selective justice--that's liberals in your family who made you miserable/mixed up.

The leftist doesn't believe he knows better, he knows he IS better so any critics are evil, dangerous, inferior.

Liberal Enemies: Attacking Trump and their own unworkable agendas are their only design for 2020.

Rape isn't a culture in America but a tragedy that happens everywhere--but victims can object here.

Obvious question: If Islam is so fantastic why is it that Muslims always come to Christian lands?

THE COMMUNIST SPIRIT

Sticky fingers is now acceptable--Overton Window has moved and stealing is now the default setting.

They take everything not nailed down whether they need it or not. Keep all valuables locked up.

Must change your posture vis-a-vis the world: medium chill, warm steel, locked gate and staying high.

RESTORE OLD PATHS

So now, join the rich and famous: don't trust anyone. You're now a target for kidnapping and ransom.

You don't deserve it in the communist spirit. Everything has to be equal so it's not fair, hand it over.

The communist spirit is here: They deserve what you have or it's "not fair".

PEOPLE: Gifts bring rifts and things attract thieves.

California times fifty is how the Democrats will have permanent political power.

They saw nothing wrong with the crude slut cuz she said she's good tho' no morals and a heart of wood.

MENTAL DROUGHTS & SENSUAL THOUGHTS

It was such an emotional and mental draught that I clung to sensual appetites just to have my own thoughts.

Society only acknowledges science which is politically correct--that race/gender are mere social constructs.

They seek social justice at the expense of truth. For an empirical scientist in this generation it's cruel.

As Overton Window is kicked hard left, a "progressive" isn't regarded anymore as radical communist.

Dumbed women adopt the dominant liberal narrative OR the one they see which is socially acceptable.

Is your wife a democrat--does she believe in (hasn't walked away) infanticide and things like that?

In WWII women were the best Nazis and in Russia they were the most ardent communists--yet you trust?

Now that social justice is the default moral position, what do we see? Women chanting what they're told.

RESTORE OLD PATHS

Decent women must lecture females on acceptable moral positions to have and what is despicably bad.

They called me angry hater cuz I had auto-immune reactions against the debauched witch on the block.

We're no longer allowed our auto-immune reactions to creeps. What used to be obvious is not to peeps.

Just because we DISCERN they call us rigid evil haters. They see ALL-AS-ONE which is a mental illness.

To be out of grace is to be on a CROOKED path. That's any sin (addiction) including to people, bad.

FAKE CHURCHES

God makes your life easier. He said He'd go before you making your crooked places straight ya hear?

God is good. The churches aren't good. Don't confuse God with men and their folderol/thinking you should.

Having seen God I'd innocently join a church. From a lamp to guide I was given a brick to carry--OUCH!

Let's do church in our homes again. Two or more gathered together, that's me and my significant others.

Blaming God for what happens in churches is stupid going against His attributes which they don't show.

Modern churches destroyed all sense of divine serenity I felt when alone with God in my sanctuary home.

Dear Lord it's the CHURCHES bringing floods of immigrants in! They are the sanctuary of demons.

The false church would want to let felons free and (to go along with things) be ok with abortion of babies.

RESTORE OLD PATHS

TRUTH PREACHES HELL/HEAVEN, SIN/REPENTANCE

The only true church preaches on hell and heaven and sin and repentance. Not "be nice" that's new age.

The less reactions you get the more you know it's God's work but not yet.

Homeless Spending has the notorious effect of doubling the homeless population like everything.

Homeless Spending notoriously doubles the homeless population as vagrants suddenly swarm in.

It should be blatantly obvious by now that progressives don't have American's best interests at heart.

"White identity is inextricably linked to violence"--how false, all we want is to be left alone you dunce.

There's a blurred line across the country against banning hate speech or banning speech they hate.

Their only option is to silence us--what a miserable admission of weakness. Jarad Taylor.

"Privilege" is actually a disadvantage as you're told to shut up by a heckling crowd, shamed and embarrassed.

Stop all your self-salvation and frenetic strife. God has already worked out the plan for your life.

God is not impressed with religion but with those believing in Him doing the impossible again and again.

They're more like preachers of a pagan socialist religion sounding more sanctimonious as time goes on.

One of their scams is to equate Christian teachings with their socialist policies and it's purely folly.

RESTORE OLD PATHS

They act like Christianity is more closely matched with good intentions not a God-centered constitution.

God-centered: God created man and his freedoms. Government is limited to allow man's gifts to come out.

THE LEFT PLAYS DIRTY POLITIX

In the secular world the left has the advantage playing dirty politics cuz the fear of the Lord restrains us.

It's charities and churches aiding and abetting illegal immigration at the border: the churches have fallen.

Illegal immigration is a systematic, coordinated, well-funded processing of people into countries for profit.

Two such myths: Borders are racist, and we're stronger the less we have in common--please resist this.

If we needed works to please God it would mean His death was not enough-- and that's blasphemous.

The reason Christianity is weak today is because the men are weak then women take over but they can't.

They fight over things because they can't use their words like men--even gangland thugs are feminine.

Not until I married a man who wouldn't take that crap did I know what a man was and I healed just like that.

THE MARVELOUS WORK AND WONDER

God puts bigger things in your spirit than you could accomplish on your own. Let em take root till full grown.

It's so big you couldn't possibly know how it's gonna happen. All you have to do is believe/be nappin'

RESTORE OLD PATHS

Trying the make things happen in our own timing is called "works of the flesh" and brings declining.

Just because God is silent doesn't mean He's given up. You may have delayed it but God hasn't denied it.

Can you trust God in the Seasons of Silence? That's the point: not seeing in the dark, but trusting.

God takes our mistakes and turns them into miracles. That is the great mercy of God and it is typical.

Our mistakes may have delayed the reward but God uses the delay to get prepared and get in accord.

Every storm surge begins with decrease. The tide goes way out--nothing--then surges--everything.

Life can be wonderful but you feel terrible due to triggered memories: This is PTSD and it plagues me.

Decades have passed, my tormenters have no idea what they did to me having no fence/always invading.

DON'T BEMOAN PAST MISTAKES

Don't bemoan past mistakes cuz had you known it wouldn't have been your fate--you had to learn escape.

When I went to lectures it was like words being poured in my brain and I felt rattled when people came.

I had reached a point of total subjectivity. My OWN reality, totally. I was in a separate reality, an anomaly.

Everything you need to fulfill your destiny is already lined up—but can be lost or warped by other people who mess up.

Just the mere fact I let em in shows I had to learn boundary issues and these were horrible lessons too.

RESTORE OLD PATHS

Don't let anyone in your home unless you know them well and don't get in cars they're goin' to hell.

They don't know what they're talking about, they have a foot in both camps--no way are they your lamp.

If I state what I think it causes shock so I'll just write it down but otherwise shut up.

WHEN YOU HAVE BUT PTSD TRASHES IT

When you have everything but still miserable you have PTSD. We all have to deal with our history.

I have everything I could want but am tormented about what you said 30 years ago, how dare you: PTSD.

My mind, tho' in final safety, would trigger back to 30 years ago and it was constant: PTSD.

When marital arguments hit on the second spouse but it's really about the first spouse, that's PTSD.

Trauma--emotional trauma of the deepest kind--locks into the system and is projected on others around.

Anorexics are so imposed on by the big bad world they do anything to create their own little world.

Every time they opened their mouth I felt imposed on. Every time they talked they wasted my time.

This was in the nineties which was SOCIAL-SOCIAL-SOCIAL before we knew what we know now.

If someone knocked on your door and you didn't let them in, that was "RUDE"--like you were expected to.

Whereas in my matrix, if someone knocks they're the rude ones if not announcing themselves first.

RESTORE OLD PATHS

After decades of this feeling of holding back a tidal wave, I finally have a fence and locked gate, hurray.

No one knows like I do what it's like to be borderless. On top of that crowded conditions is disastrous.

With a fence and locked gate no one knows I exist but that's so much better than flooded with twits.

YOU DON'T JUST GET THE PERSON

You don't just get the person. You get them, their stuff, their family, friends and habits so I'd forget em.

One therapy for PTSD is being mindful of the present. Hear the birds or music instead of thinking back.

You imposed on me so much--my spirit cried out but I had to learn assertion, that's why it was allowed.

You get them, their stuff, friends, family, habits, routines, viewpoints--no thanks.

There's nothing I can do with another rather than alone which I prefer.

The best marriages nurture each other's privacy. You're not together all the time, you're alone mostly.

The spouse keeps people away--acting as a fence--so the other can grow in selfhood and abundance.

He keeps people away so I'm free to develop on my own accord. No outside influences to hurt anymore.

The bible is clear about wicked men hypnotizing weak women in their homes--the horrors of being alone.

My home is MY sanctuary--do they treat it as such? Or come in to confront me and bore me so much.

RESTORE OLD PATHS

The idea of someone getting a bee in their bonnet and coming to your home to confront you on it? Forget it!

HOME RULES NOT TAUGHT IN SCHOOLS

Hardly anyone knows how to act in your home. You gotta train em unless they're from days of old.

It's so horrible how they act it's hard to imagine. You can't even conger it and they keep pushing limits.

With prevalent sin (all barriers down) comes wrath: anger, violence, treachery towards family and friends.

Don't let anyone in if they come angry or frettin'. That's your sanctuary and it's about SPIRITS: demons.

You must vet everyone who comes to your house. It's about spirits and the fact that contact = conquest.

I was terrified of my unwanted guests, fearing what they'd do if I didn't let em in but they destroyed it soon.

Appeasement never works when dealing with Hitlers or mobs of unruly monsters so call the sheriff.

Even the church ladies believed in these things like pagan rituals, witchcraft, reincarnation or homos.

I couldn't find my bearings with anyone around. Just dogs, cats and my desert walks with nature's sounds.

There's nothing I can do with another when alone isn't better.

Instead of seeking to please everyone, prepare for that ONE then you'll have victory/you've won.

With PTSD one disassociates from his environment–it becomes hazy as energy is pulled instead to memory.

So the cure for bad memories is to connect to your own environment--IN SITU: in your magic situation.

Lord is known by the judgment he executes: the wicked is ensnared in the work of his own hands. Psa 9:16

Having no appreciation for difference in thought is **NOT** true diversity but that's the liberal lies we bought.

HOLY SPIRIT EASE: GOD SMOOTHES THINGS OUT

After struggling for decades I assumed that's the way it always would be until supernatural grace: ease.

I assumed I'd always be working 18 hours a day but that was just that phase now it's Holy Spirit Ease.

Divine favor doesn't just come in riches but lightening the load and taking the pressure off: that's GOD!

I can't just talk about the good--that's stupid! Both sides must be described so you can avoid the hoods.

Bible describes creepy people all through it. Only the false New Age calls em good tho' they screw up.

We're told to love creepy people but hate God who made us all: this is the new age, worshipping rabble.

God smoothes things out. You're gonna come into a season where things fall into place: amazing, wow!

He anoints my head with oil: OIL makes things flow easily, things that are stuck--breakthrough is my God.

God is gonna oil your life. This anointing will cause things to be easier and free of that awful demon: strife.

In this new season you'll accomplish more with less effort. New attractions flow in to team your endeavor.

RESTORE OLD PATHS

What stopped you in the past and caused friction won't stop you anymore, you're into success forever.

LIFE WILL ACTUALLY BE EASY

You'll accomplish GREAT things then think "this was so much easier than I thought": that's God's EASE.

The difficulty/onerousness of tasks was just a phase in the preparatory stage coming up to success.

Father: Thank you that your yoke is easy, that you're equipped me and empowered me.

The past was struggle, strain and difficulty. But I learned God's Ease says that isn't how it should be.

I came into the Anointing of Ease where what once was a struggle wasn't anymore, I was free.

Quit spelling defeat! It's a new day of oiled strength cuz you weren't created to struggle your whole life.

With supernatural power it will be EASY to break an addiction, it will be EASY to break from bad friends.

"THEY'RE ALL GOOD" IS MALICIOUS FALSEHOOD

Let em go, these people will be cut off--destroyed, God said. "They're all good" is malicious falsehood.

PRESSURE to pay the bills, pressure to get ahead, pressure to sell books: that all came to an end!

New doors will open and your gifts and talents will be released in a new way. Just learn about people, sorry:

Face it. Evil sisters, evil brothers, evil father and mother. Release it: God said we're all rags/none better.

RESTORE OLD PATHS

I'm none better than a filthy rag. The only thing giving status is loving my Father in Heaven, my Dad.

Good breaks will find me, talents will be discovered, new doors will open so I'll reject evil old ones.

God has the right people lined up for you. Right opportunities: tho' you haven't seen it yet it's true.

GOD TAKES THE PRESSURE OFF

To take the pressure off God will do something unusual, something unexpected and entirely unpredicted.

In a world beyond gross you stand out as The Most. That'll make it a cakewalk to rise up to your best.

We expect it to be difficult, we expect to fail. Turn it around: Father thanks for Your anointing to prevail.

Watch out for stupid people because they get violent too. High IQ brings restraint but it's only a few.

God will put you in the right place at the right time. He will open doors no man can shut cuz He's sublime.

God causes people to want to be good to you. Out of nowhere you're rewarded when works is through.

If it's onerous or daunting, say "this isn't permanent, ease is coming". Repeat that whenever stalling.

When God fights your battles He puts pressure on those having what's yours--spears traded for plowshares.

Harvest, final breakthrough, healing, season of ease--whatever you want to call it it's the Garden of Eden.

God'll get it all back cuz if it has your name on it, it's YOURS--that's a fact as you'll soon see so relax.

RESTORE OLD PATHS

He'll give you the victory without you even having to fight. Freedom belongs to you, wholeness, victory too.

I'll never get well, it's too hard: This yoke of bondage is being broken this minute, prepare to win it.

IT'S A NEW DAY, HURRAY!

It's a NEW DAY: You're getting a yoke of ease, a yoke of freedom, a strife-free world without these demons.

Suddenly God moved me from danger to wonderful new neighbors but I expected similar disfavor.

My SEASONS had changed but I expected the same old/same old fair-weather friends so deranged.

I was so used to being misunderstood, taken out of context or gossiped about I didn't realize my luck.

Even the churches would spout the liberal narrative in my home and I thought Lord, please get rid of em.

Even churches would go along with this crap about open borders and a better life, to hell with us inside.

WOMEN FEEL SORRY

Women feel sorry for everyone but us. They pity homosexuals, border invaders, the whole world can come.

Women are LIBERALS, please take their vote away! I'd gladly give up mine if America could stay OK.

Ever since "Deep Throat" blow jobs is all they talk about. Lil' old ladies, dear uncles have all flipped out.

Natural sex is perverted through tolerance and it's a mess as innocents are expected to adapt to it.

RESTORE OLD PATHS

He labels himself "philosopher, writer" but never said a thing but dribble or repeating the narrative.

Parents: Do NOT let your kids into locked rooms. Do NOT let their guests bring your home into doom.

FREAKS: YOUR KID'S GUESTS ARE SICK

Your kid's guests are sick. Recognize that and nip it in the bud! Organize your home like a Swiss clock.

Search your kid's room. If you find ANY porn you must search it like a prison guard and then burn it.

Pornography is Satan sitting in the wings ready to destroy your family. It's a demon from hell so be ready.

When I found porn in the home it so shocked me I wished I had never been born but God's goodness I adore.

What kid is strong enough to reject porn when he sees it? Tell em about the brain--how it shrinks it.

You tried in the past and it didn't work out. Try again cuz you're in a new season and God is your Father.

You don't have to do it in your own strength cuz God is fighting your battles. Declare: I have won it all.

Sorry girl it's not you, it's your husband. Yuk three times, I don't blame you for who you're married to.

God is NOT "all-loving". His all-lovingness is the biggest lie of the devil ever told to the innocents.

God hated Esau and He hated all workers of iniquity. He said don't even dine with those who hate Me.

Jesus didn't come to "UNITE" which sounds so nice but is BS. He came to DIVIDE the evil from us.

RESTORE OLD PATHS

THESE PEOPLE ARE NOT YOUR FRIENDS

These people are not your friends and never were. They came to use you for everything you have or are.

While nappin': the problem you thought would NEVER turn around, SUDDENLY you'll see it all happen.

NO you can't use my washer, go to the laundromat. NO you aren't invited for dinner, we have plans.

The biggest problem making you down on your luck is being STUCK to muck: chumps on your couch.

God is working behind the scenes lining up what you need. You'll never have to struggle in the New Season.

GOD ALWAYS GIVES YOU ESCAPE

You may have been in a difficult time but God is about to take the pressure off! What a change, what relief.

When God rescued me I gained a strength I never had before. People went out of their way/came forth.

When God came in old crutches and enablers dissolved away. It just happened, nothing I could say.

Yoke of bondage is coming off, the yoke of ease is coming on--like changing clothes or going home.

What's hindered you in the past is not gonna hinder you in the future--a whole new change for sure.

So the Elect stays in pink: You're gonna overcome obstacles/achieve dreams easier than you think.

A false teacher [not there yet] will take you so far then get jealous but true teachers are proud of ya.

RESTORE OLD PATHS

Once narcissist finds what he wants he will monopolize you and worm his way to all aspects of your life.

White libs so desperate to be seen as anti-racist they vote in bigots and loonies from immigrant communities.

EVIL FREAKS: BEYOND GROSS

I'm so excited by my new book: EVIL FREAKS (BEYOND GROSS). It's all about liberalism, ya know.

German part of me: scholarly, scientific, attention to detail with complexity and great organization.

Scotch part of me: Love of the Lord, religious, familial, into solitude and privacy with a MOLT around me.

Finish your work, put it up. It's there--they just have yet to see it, that's all. Wait, pray, continue on.

I'm into the STEM--of religious protestant Calvinist zealots--not these creepy evil offshoots in the pits.

I'm not at all interested in a windfall but justified remuneration and recognition for the work of my hands.

If you're heavy on feeling element you must control the precious mind or you've had it, it congers up.

In an earlier season of my life I had to put up with people and that was my Ph.D. in the streets, horrible.

I had to adapt to their insanity when I knew they didn't (couldn't) understand me. It was surrealistic.

You have to write with a mind only to the truth, not whether they'll like or agree with it--can you do that?

I see the light at the end of the tunnel and it's simply unbelievable as I snap in the last piece of the puzzle.

RESTORE OLD PATHS

In every project there's a beginning, a middle and an end. There IS an end, an evident completion.

When is the END? When it meets the link.

One NEVER knows when he will be done until he is done. Albert Einstein

YOUR TORMENTERS ARE OLD MEN NOW

Your tormenters are old men now--just stealing/dealing bums--cuz God your Father cut em off.

I won't judge him, all I know is: I go to sleep around him.

When your time has come the right link will show up. Don't stress cuz it will find you no matter what.

There will be a grace that causes things to fall into place.

I call it a witch when it's like this. Not home-centered, filled with sins and you couldn't care less, adrift.

If heavy on the feeling element you really gotta watch what your mind congers up--keep the mind straight.

I must maintain my reality because I know what happens when I lose it, and it's hell beneath/can't breathe.

I will not listen to them nor respond to them. No matter where they're coming from, I'm retired/DONE.

I've done my work, a lot more than most. It will stand on its own long after I'm dead and gone I hope.

My whole development came from successive eliminations: of people, habits and now foods. Purification.

If heavy on the feeing element watch what mind congers up and staying away from those bringing it up.

RESTORE OLD PATHS

I just tell em I have a sick husband at home and they don't charge me thinking they're next in line.

The only thing separating me from heaven is body/memories. I wish it were healthy/they were gone.

I don't wanna be worshipped but those people gave me NO support and even put it all down/dismissed it.

Quit thinking about what coulda happened and just what DID happen: You got away/escaped, you're ok.

LIBERALISM IS CAPTURED BY PROJECTIONS

Liberalism: It was frightening to be captured by his projections then to become a slave to it all.

All of a sudden and by pure magic coincidence the limelight will be on you so PREPARE/be ready too.

You can be conquered and possessed by someone just as easily on the net, you know. Cut ties/just say NO.

I'm in the groove, doing my thing as God directs. No one's gonna interfere with that: bad advice is a hex.

The reason you went through all that is you hadn't learned the lesson yet and when you did, hell with it.

Stop reliving the awful past--realize there are SEASONS of your life and that was a much lower level.

I had to go through ALL THAT--excruciating things--to learn the lesson of boundaries, walls and lines.

Without a fence people impose themselves on you and its HELL--gotta stop em at the gate with a bell.

Stop reliving the awful past--realize there are SEASONS of life and that one was preparing for strife.

RESTORE OLD PATHS

How could I have learned about borders and the awfulness of the kids bringing in others calling us haters?

Because I didn't want to "socialize" (hang out) they targeted me for daring to be independent and free.

GROWING MUSCLE FROM RESISTANCE

We grow muscle through resistance and those kids provided it--evil stepmother syndrome was part of it.

What I endured by my invaders was so horrible it was like being in jail: it either makes you great or failed.

Evil Stepmother Syndrome: The projection-archetype of the "evil other" cuz she's not their mother.

From an insecure weakling to social muscle: that's what I gained from solitude--mastery, adroit, supple.

As a HERO falling, it compelled them to rise up against you. That's the system in the bible all through.

Arrogance precedes ruin and the devastation can last for decades in the desert wilderness, but that ENDS.

You were weak (a filthy sinner) and that attracted their beak (rising up against you): a system no-brainer.

Once the Creative Act is complete it attracts pollination. The link just appears--a natural part of completion.

No more work/books read. For when you don't work you relax into inspiration instead.

IMMUNITY IS IN THE GUT

80% of immune system is in the gut. Auto-immune disease: drop dairy, grains, nightshades for a.

RESTORE OLD PATHS

Just ONE change in diet and your whole life transforms! Acid-burn is GONE after deleting what harms.

All my life especially as a fruitarian I ate salsa and all my life I suffered with acid burn in the esophagus.

Tomatoes, potatoes, peppers, citrus, coffee, processed foods caused excruciating pain.

I dropped those foods and INSTANTLY the pain was gone. My esophagus healed, thank you God.

Potatoes seemed so "soft" and soothing, was raised on em, but pain from nightshades was the problem.

They sell products to restore the gut of course but I think that if you just delete these foods you'll be buff.

With age comes poorer circulation which means the ends dry out. Use Lanolin the best moisturizer of all.

The answer to all diets is to constantly change your diet. Man/dog are omnivores, they can do it.

EAT CALORICALLY DENSE ONCE A DAY

I couldn't let veganism go mentally--even though my poor body had rejected the silly notion entirely.

I need dense calories once a day, that's all. When I live on high fat/sugar/starch I'm high and having a ball.

Keep your lowcarb diet, I need HIGH carb man. To live without carbs, sugar and lotsa fat I'm dull/bland.

By including cheese, cream and butter my health snapped back instantly after the vegan deficiencies.

I have butter or cheese every day--everything is shiny and well-oiled and all deficiencies stay away.

RESTORE OLD PATHS

Who wants to eat sparse calories–fruits and veggies--all day long? I'm telling you after 20 years it got old.

Besides fruit smoothies I don't even eat produce now. Just ONE meal of dense calories/butter is all I know.

GET SOME CLASS IN THE KITCHEN

Why would I eat your chili when you kept tasting from the spoon you stirred it with, wake up witch.

Eat real foods cuz they go through, the processed stuff sticks like glue.

The ice cream drumstick hit like lead twelve hours later my poor stomach said.

Why would I wanna eat your spaghetti Twit when you kept tasting the sauce from the spoon you stirred it with?

They taste from the spoon and put it back in the pot! I see this all the time in a culture going to rot.

Though a woman's behind is supposed to be like an apple not a pear, maybe not that much!

I can eat some citrus so how about tangerines for breakfast, shrimp for lunch and no dinner of course.

Avoid sickening concoctions they make and just eat whole foods like God made in their original state.

In dropping problem foods I instantly deflated. It was such a relief! Obstruction gone/got back my energy.

AUTOIMMUNE RESPONSES ARE AN ATTACK

The body ATTACKED foods it saw as an allergen. It was hell being trapped in this leaky gut syndrome.

First day in decades that I didn't take Rolaids or Alka-Seltzer to quiet the pain.

RESTORE OLD PATHS

Entire cultures are food-based on nightshades. Potato continents or tomatoes over everything: violence?

I think I can still eat my favorite fruit tangerines, but we'll have to see. The pain is hours later, searing.

I'm deflating as bothersome upper hip bumps from the dairy is daily dissolving, they were unnerving.

It's not just dairy/grains but nightshades creating leaky gut as the S-H-I-T seeps through to bloodstream.

Tomatoes seem harmless, potatoes seem comfy but these nightshades have ruined whole countries.

Whole CONTINENTS live on potatoes or tomatoes--the implications culturally are amazing to think about.

Dairy, grains and nightshades are ok for some but with autoimmune leaky gut you gotta delete em all.

Dizziness, bloat, pessimism, lost goals, billiousness, fatigue, lost hopes all came from my LEAKY GUT.

Leaky gut: The only way to keep fecal matter outa the blood is to delete whole categories of food stuffs.

PRESSURES OF AUTOIMMUNITY

Pressures of autoimmunity: You reacting all the time cuz everything is bad while they have seared consciences.

Just as I auto-react to wrong foods I react RIGHTLY to crude dudes but I'm called unloving by fools.

People gotta watch what they say. If a woman is gross, callous, unfeeling, dogmatic it shows right away.

It is horrifying how dense and callous they are. They call themselves loving while we tear out our hair.

94

RESTORE OLD PATHS

Pressures of autoimmunity: Like being a cat in a room full of rocking-chairs.

All I can do is get back into music, another groove. Politix videos brings more frustration that I ever knew.

Truth: What holds us down? SIN and SINNERS--prune your network.

100 KAREN KELLOCK BOOKS

AFFINITY OR MISERY
AGELESS CORNUCOPIA
AMERICA AWAKE!
AMERICA'S DAFT ERA
ARTS OF PALEO FASTING
AUTOPHAGY ON CHEATERS
BACKSTABBING NEUROTICS
BETRAYAL TRAUMA
BOOMERS AND BROKENNESS
BOOT ON NECK
CHAMPION GUIDES
COMMIE NUTHOUSE
COMMIES
COMMUNIST SPIRIT
CONTAGION OF MADNESS
CONTAGIOUS MADNESS
CULTURE CLASH BASHED
DAFT LEFT
DAILY FASTARIAN
DAM RATS
DIVERSITY IS CRUELTY
E-RACE WHITE
EVIL FREAKS (Beyond Gross)
THE END OR A BEND?
FEMALE BULLIES AND FEMI-NAZIS
FEMALE CARNALITY
FEMALE DUMB DOWN
FEMALE POWER DRIVE
FEMINISM AND RUIN 1 & 2
FIX FOR MISFITS
FOOLS & TRAMPS
FREEDOM SPEAKING
FRENEMY ENABLER
FRENEMY LIAR
FRENEMY THIEF
FRENEMY TRAITOR
TRENEMY TYRANT
GENIUS IS HELD DOWN
GLOBALISLAM
GOD USES THE FLAWED
HAZE OF THE LATTER DAYS

THE HERD IN WORDS
HIX POLITIX
HOW THEY RUINED US
JUST SKIP DINNER
LE FEMME AND THE COMMUNIST SPIRIT
LIBERAL CHAOS & ROT
LIBERAL DOUBLETHINK
LIBERAL GALL 1 & 2
LIBERAL SHOVE-DOWNS
LOCK YOUR GATE
LOSERS and Femme Fatales
MANUAL FOR SUPERIOR MEN
MODERN ART FROM HELL
MOSTLY FAKE
NOTES TO CHAMPS 1 & 2
OVERCOME FRENEMIES
PC MAKES US CRAZY
PEOPLE ARE CRUEL
PEOPLE PROBLEMS 1 & 2
PERSECUTED GENIUIS
POLI-PSYCH MYSTERIES
PRETENTIOUS SLOBS
QUEEN BEE
RED NEW DEAL
RETURNING TO FIRST NATURE
SEASON OF TREASON
SEPARATE MEANS HOLY
SOCIAL HYPNOTISM
SOLITUDE SOLUTION
SUPERCILIOUS
THE SCHOOLS SCREWED EM UP
TOAD TO PRINCE
TRIALS CYCLES
TRUMP VS. GROUP
TRUST IN TRASH
THE TRUTH ABOUT PEOPLE
UNDERHEANDEDLY CLEVER
WALK TALL WITHIN WALLS
WE'RE NOT ALL ONE
WINNERS SKIP DINNER
WORK OR SMERK

KAREN KELLOCK PH.D.

M.S. Political Science, San Diego State. Ph.D. in Psychology, University of California Irvine. Postdoctoral: UCI School of Medicine, Dept. of Psychiatry [NIMH Grants]. Developed the Debris Theory of Disease, a theory of system pathology in 120 books and 22 textbooks for the general public. The theory has a general formula: All disease is obstruction, all recovery is elimination, all success is attraction. The three obstructions are people, habit and food. Remove obstruction and snap to your goals, waiting in the wings.

·